One
*Healing the
Racial Divide*

Dennis Rouse

STUDY GUIDE

One
Healing the Racial Divide

Dennis Rouse

STUDY GUIDE

Contents

Starting Point

"At that moment, I had the stark realization that I had absolutely no comprehension of the pain she felt in a prejudiced society that put black people in a subservient place. I didn't have a clue what they faced. Her heart was melted by our simple invitation, and my heart was broken by the profound sadness she continually experienced. I was determined to do something about it, but I had no idea what steps I could take."

Reading Time

Read Chapter 1: "Starting Point," in *One*, reflect on the questions and discuss your answers with your study group.

Reflect on the culture in which you grew up. Did you experience a relatively integrated community, or were you surrounded primarily with those of your own racial/ethnic background?

_____

_____

_____

_____

_____

_____

When do you first remember recognizing that others' experiences were different from your own? How did this experience change you?

_____

_____

_____

_____

_____

_____

Study Scripture

Read Matthew 20:20-28:

"Then the mother of Zebedee's sons came to Jesus with her sons and, kneeling down, asked a favor of him.

'What is it you want?' he asked.

She said, 'Grant that one of these two sons of mine may sit at your right and the other at your left in your kingdom.'

'You don't know what you are asking,' Jesus said to them. 'Can you drink the cup I am going to drink?'

Jesus said to them, 'You will indeed drink from my cup, but to sit at my right or left is not for me to grant. These places belong to those for whom they have been prepared by my Father.'

When the ten heard about this, they were indignant with the two brothers. Jesus called them together and said, 'You know that the rulers of the Gentiles lord it over them, and their high officials exercise authority over them. Not so with you. Instead, whoever wants to become great among you must be your servant, and whoever wants to be first must be your slave— just as the Son of Man did not come to be served, but to serve, and to give his life as a ransom for many.'"

How do we see Jesus giving away His life—and His power—for the sake of others in this passage?

_____

_____

_____

_____

According to Chapter 1, what is the common experience around which all of us—no matter our background—are called to unite?

_____

_____

_____

_____

What's the difference between different people groups being in the same room and being part of the same family?

_____

_____

_____

_____

What negative side effects do you see in Dennis's account of the forced integration he experienced in his school years? Where do you think this policy went wrong? Was there anything positive about it?

_____

_____

_____

_____

_____

_____

Share Your Story

"Proximity forces us to stop, engage, listen, and try to understand the other side of every argument."

How does proximity challenge us to recognize the views and experiences of others in new ways?

_____

_____

_____

_____

_____

_____

How does the kingdom culture that Christ brought balance personal responsibility and compassion for the disadvantaged?

_____

_____

_____

_____

_____

_____

What challenges might true, Biblical reconciliation initially pose for people of color, who haven't historically been in a place of power?

_____

_____

_____

_____

_____

_____

_____

What challenges might true, Biblical reconciliation initially pose for white people, who are used to being in the position of power?

_____

_____

_____

_____

After reading this chapter, how is the Holy Spirit leading you to respond? What research, relationships, or other actions do you feel led to pursue?

_____

_____

_____

_____

It's Not Fair

"If we know Him . . . if His love has melted and molded our hearts . . . we'll give more honor to others, we'll be interested in their problems, and we'll devote ourselves to help them rise higher. That's what it means to be motivated by love to make adjustments for others' sake."

Reading Time

Read Chapter 2:
"It's Not Fair,"
in *One*, reflect
on the questions
and discuss your
answers with your
study group.

Do you feel comfortable engaging in conversation with people who have different backgrounds than you? How easily do you welcome views and perspectives that don't align with your own?

_____

_____

_____

_____

_____

_____

What's the danger in pinning the "Christian label" onto one party, race, ethnicity, or people group? How does this hinder the kingdom reconciliation God wants to advance in and through us?

_____

_____

_____

_____

_____

_____

Study Scripture

Read Colossians 3:1-14:

"Since, then, you have been raised with Christ, set your hearts on things above, where Christ is, seated at the right hand of God. Set your minds on things above, not on earthly things. For you died, and your life is now hidden with Christ in God. When Christ, who is your life, appears, then you also will appear with him in glory.

Put to death, therefore, whatever belongs to your earthly nature: sexual immorality, impurity, lust, evil desires and greed, which is idolatry. Because of these, the wrath of God is coming. You used to walk in these ways, in the life you once lived. But now you must also rid yourselves of all such things as these: anger, rage, malice, slander, and filthy language from your lips. Do not lie to each other, since you have taken off your old self with its practices and have put on the new self, which is being renewed in knowledge in the image of its Creator. Here there is no Gentile or Jew, circumcised or uncircumcised, barbarian, Scythian, slave or free, but Christ is all, and is in all.

Therefore, as God's chosen people, holy and dearly loved, clothe yourselves with compassion, kindness, humility, gentleness and patience. Bear with each other and forgive one another if any of you has a grievance against someone. Forgive as the Lord forgave you. And over all these virtues put on love, which binds them all together in perfect unity."

How have earthly values taken the church away from this mindset? Where have we compromised a Biblical view of the kingdom in favor of a biased, preferential perspective?

_____

_____

_____

_____

How does the kingdom viewpoint in this passage free us to embrace and understand the perspectives of those who are not like us?

_____

_____

_____

_____

People of all backgrounds have the propensity to see themselves either as entitled or as victims. What are the dangers in either viewpoint?

_____

_____

_____

_____

_____

How many true friends do you have from races/ethnicities other than your own? What steps do you need to take to increase your relationships with those of other backgrounds?

_____

_____

_____

_____

_____

Share Your Story

"Love is being willing to make adjustments for another person... in our relationships with people of other races, we make adjustments to lay our presumptions aside and value them as much as God values us."

Do you tend to view those on the other side of the political divide as foolish or evil? How do you tend to feel towards them in general?

_____

_____

_____

_____

_____

_____

How has social media and virtual interaction with others contributed to the division, hatred, anger, and prejudice in our society? Is there anything unifying about it?

_____

_____

_____

_____

_____

_____

According to Chapter 2, what is the only thing that can melt our hearts to the point where we are motivated to make adjustments for others' sake? Why won't anything else work?

_____

_____

_____

_____

_____

_____

Do you currently find yourself in a radical position, a moderate position, or a confused position when it comes to racial issues? Explain your answer.

_____

_____

_____

_____

_____

What adjustments is the Holy Spirit calling you to make for others, in light of the immense sacrifices that God has made for you?

_____

_____

_____

_____

_____

Why Preference Seems Reasonable

"Many of us secretly see our race as "better than," "more responsible than," and "more noble than," but we don't say it out loud. We just prefer to be with people who look like us, cook like us, talk like us, and see the world the way we do. It's much more comfortable that way."

Read Chapter 3:
"Why Preference
Seems Reasonable,"
in *One*, reflect
on the questions
and discuss your
answers with your
study group.

How do you think the traditions you grew with have kept you from asking hard questions?

_____

_____

_____

_____

_____

_____

What are some examples of "entrenched inequality" in our communities? How have our systems and structures normalized this inequality?

_____

_____

_____

_____

_____

_____

Study Scripture

Read James 1:19-27:

"My dear brothers and sisters, take note of this: Everyone should be quick to listen, slow to speak and slow to become angry, because human anger does not produce the righteousness that God desires. Therefore, get rid of all moral filth and the evil that is so prevalent and humbly accept the word planted in you, which can save you.

Do not merely listen to the word, and so deceive yourselves. Do what it says. Anyone who listens to the word but does not do what it says is like someone who looks at his face in a mirror and, after looking at himself, goes away and immediately forgets what he looks like. But whoever looks intently into the perfect law that gives freedom, and continues in it—not forgetting what they have heard, but doing it—they will be blessed in what they do.

Those who consider themselves religious and yet do not keep a tight rein on their tongues deceive themselves, and their religion is worthless. Religion that God our Father accepts as pure and faultless is this: to look after orphans and widows in their distress and to keep oneself from being polluted by the world."

When we adopt the middle position of "preference," how are our words different from our heart-level beliefs and opinions?

_____

_____

_____

_____

_____

Is there any area of your life in which you profess to believe one thing, but don't act in accordance with that belief?

_____

_____

_____

_____

_____

Which of the five responses to racial inequality stands out to you the most? Why do you think this is?

_____

_____

_____

_____

_____

If you had to choose one of the five that most closely represents where you are today, which one would you honestly choose? Explain your answer.

_____

_____

_____

_____

_____

Share Your Story

"The solution to racism and intolerance isn't passive preference. That's not good enough."

Is there anything in particular holding you back from moving "up" the list towards inclusion? What is it?

_____

_____

_____

_____

_____

_____

How does preference appear deceivingly tolerant while actually sustaining the prejudices and comfort of those in its grasp?

_____

_____

_____

_____

_____

_____

How has the media added to the division between whites and people of color? Are there any ways media has helped to bridge this divide?

_____

_____

_____

_____

_____

_____

Why isn't passive preference good enough as a solution to racism? How is it a step ahead of blatant racism and intolerance?

_____

_____

_____

_____

_____

What is your perspective on the generational differences between your generation and those older/younger than you?

_____

_____

_____

_____

_____

Is there anything God is leading you to take action on after reading this chapter?

_____

_____

_____

_____

_____

chapter 4

Love Conquers All

"I'm convinced that many of us are far more influenced by the world's values than God's values. I also believe there are unseen forces at work: forces of light and forces of darkness. The forces of light invite us to love like Jesus loves; the forces of darkness sow negative assumptions which quickly turn hearts cold. Which side is reflected in our attitudes, our behavior, our words, and our posts?"

Reading Time

Read Chapter 4: "Love Conquers All," in *One*, reflect on the questions and discuss your answers with your study group.

How does offense hold us back from reconciliation with others?

_____

_____

_____

_____

_____

_____

_____

Do you find yourself struggling with anger, divisiveness, and unforgiveness towards anyone currently? If so, who is it?

_____

_____

_____

_____

_____

_____

_____

Study Scripture

Read 2 Corinthians 5:14-21:

"For Christ's love compels us, because we are convinced that one died for all, and therefore all died. And he died for all, that those who live should no longer live for themselves but for him who died for them and was raised again.

So from now on we regard no one from a worldly point of view. Though we once regarded Christ in this way, we do so no longer. Therefore, if anyone is in Christ, the new creation has come: The old has gone, the new is here! All this is from God, who reconciled us to himself through Christ and gave us the ministry of reconciliation: that God was reconciling the world to himself in Christ, not counting people's sins against them. And he has committed to us the message of reconciliation. We are therefore Christ's ambassadors, as though God were making his appeal through us. We implore you on Christ's behalf: Be reconciled to God. God made him who had no sin to be sin for us, so that in him we might become the righteousness of God."

Why is it necessary for us to be reconciled to God before we can reconcile with others?

_____

_____

_____

_____

_____

How does Christ model the kind of reconciliation we need in our world today?

_____

_____

_____

_____

_____

Of the four dimensions of love discussed in this chapter, which one do you currently struggle with the most? Why do you think this is?

_____

_____

_____

_____

_____

Why do you think so many go to church for years but never experience a heart-transforming encounter with Jesus Christ? Are there any aspects of church culture that contribute to this?

_____

_____

_____

_____

_____

Why can't government be the ultimate solution for racial tensions and for equity? What role does the government need to play in these areas?

_____

_____

_____

_____

_____

_____

What was your reaction to Pastor Dennis's account of washing the feet of the black man onstage? What did you think of the audience's reactions?

_____

_____

_____

_____

_____

_____

What is the difference between holding onto offense and feeling hurt/anger/indignation over a wrong?

_____

_____

_____

_____

_____

_____

_____

Do you think it's possible to live in a perpetual state of forgiveness? Explain your answer.

_____

_____

_____

_____

_____

What group or groups do you find difficult to see as being in the image of God? Is it another race/ethnicity? Another culture? A certain political party or religion?

_____

_____

_____

_____

_____

Equal?

"To move beyond preference and paternalism, we must see people as equals. Superiority of any kind, even if it motivates us to give generously to cross-cultural causes, still leaves a barrier between us and them."

Reading Time

Read Chapter 5: "Equal?" in *One*, reflect on the questions and discuss your answers with your study group.

How do self-righteousness and pride hold us back from hold us back from seeing ourselves as we truly are? How do they hold us back from loving others in their imperfections?

_____

_____

_____

_____

_____

Are you relatively comfortable in being open about your flaws and failures to others? What, if anything, makes vulnerability challenging for you?

_____

_____

_____

_____

_____

Study Scripture

Read Matthew 25:31-46:

"When the Son of Man comes in his glory, and all the angels with him, he will sit on his glorious throne. All the nations will be gathered before him, and he will separate the people one from another as a shepherd separates the sheep from the goats. He will put the sheep on his right and the goats on his left.

"Then the King will say to those on his right, 'Come, you who are blessed by my Father; take your inheritance, the kingdom prepared for you since the creation of the world. For I was hungry and you gave me something to eat, I was thirsty and you gave me something to drink, I was a stranger and you invited me in, I needed clothes and you clothed me, I was sick and you looked after me, I was in prison and you came to visit me.'

"Then the righteous will answer him, 'Lord, when did we see you hungry and feed you, or thirsty and give you something to drink? When did we see you a stranger and invite you in, or needing clothes and clothe you? When did we see you sick or in prison and go to visit you?'

"The King will reply, 'Truly I tell you, whatever you did for one of the least of these brothers and sisters of mine, you did for me.'

"Then he will say to those on his left, 'Depart from me, you who are cursed, into the eternal fire prepared for the devil and his angels. For I was hungry and you gave me nothing to eat, I was thirsty and you gave me nothing to drink, I was a stranger and you did not invite me in, I needed clothes and you did not clothe me, I was sick and in prison and you did not look after me.'

"They also will answer, 'Lord, when did we see you hungry or thirsty or a stranger or needing clothes or sick or in prison, and did not help you?'

"He will reply, 'Truly I tell you, whatever you did not do for one of the least of these, you did not do for me.'

"Then they will go away to eternal punishment, but the righteous to eternal life."

How did the King evaluate the sheep and the goats? How is this different from the way we might evaluate them?

_____

_____

_____

_____

_____

What message do you think Christ was sending with this story? How is this message still extremely relevant today?

_____

_____

_____

_____

_____

Can you recall a time when you realized you couldn't be enough in and of yourself? How did this experience change your perspective of others?

_____

_____

_____

_____

_____

For you, what's challenging about moving towards people who are self-destructing instead of judging or avoiding them?

_____

_____

_____

_____

_____

Why is the false niceness of white fragility actually destructive to racial equality?

_____

_____

_____

_____

_____

_____

Pastor Dennis writes, "Being nice to people to prove that we're good is only using them for our benefit." How do you think the recipients of false niceness feel when they know it's not sincere?

_____

_____

_____

_____

_____

_____

What freedom is there in admitting that we will never be enough on our own? How does this free us up to love others in a more Christ-like way?

_____

_____

_____

_____

_____

_____

Which statistic about racial disparity in the United States stood out to you the most? Explain your answer.

_____

_____

_____

_____

_____

After reading this chapter, what actions is the Holy Spirit leading you to take? How do you sense your own heart needing to be moved towards a more Biblical view of equality?

_____

_____

_____

_____

Foundation Stones

"If we lean toward righteousness, we need to ask, "What are some genuine injustices that need to be remedied?" And if we lean toward justice, we need to ask, "How can I encourage people to be responsible citizens?""

Read Chapter 6: "Foundation Stones," in *One*, reflect on the questions and discuss your answers with your study group.

Do you tend to listen mostly to news outlets, journalists, and other sources of information that align with your current views? How often do you listen to sources that don't align with your views?

_____

_____

_____

_____

_____

_____

Why do you think it's so difficult for people to admit how much they "lean to one side" of any given argument or issue?

_____

_____

_____

_____

_____

_____

Study Scripture

Read Proverbs 21:1-3:

"The king's heart is a stream of water in the hand of the LORD;
he turns it wherever he will.

Every way of a man is right in his own eyes,
but the LORD weighs the heart.

To do righteousness and justice
is more acceptable to the LORD than sacrifice.

Haughty eyes and a proud heart,
the lamp of the wicked, are sin.

The plans of the diligent lead surely to abundance,
but everyone who is hasty comes only to poverty."

Why do you think righteousness and justice are paired in this passage—
what's the significance of the Lord prizing these two things above sacrifice?

_____

_____

_____

_____

_____

_____

Do you tend to lean more towards the righteousness side of the spectrum
or the justice side? How do you know?

_____

_____

_____

_____

_____

How do righteousness and justice work together to found a strong, godly society?

_____

_____

_____

_____

_____

_____

What is confirmation bias, and how does it keep us from considering others' points of view?

_____

_____

_____

_____

_____

What's the danger of having a heart for righteousness without justice?

_____

_____

_____

_____

_____

_____

What's the danger of having a heart for justice without righteousness?

_____

_____

_____

_____

_____

_____

What are some practical ways you can move towards the other end of the righteousness/justice spectrum?

_____

_____

_____

_____

_____

_____

Think about the groups of people you find difficult to love. Can you identify any relationships you have with these people currently? If not, how can you move towards cultivating or deepening connections with them?

_____

_____

_____

_____

_____

_____

Are there any other action steps you feel God leading you to take as you finish this chapter? What about verses or other points that stood out to you?

_____

_____

_____

_____

_____

_____

Crazy Love

"When we love our enemies, pray for those who persecute us, and bless those who cruelly use us, we're like God. We need to remember that we were His enemies, we worshipped created things instead of the Creator, and we used people instead of loving them ... but the love of God is so great that He loved us still. That's the deep well of love we can draw from: we love others the way God loves us."

Read Chapter 7:
"Crazy Love," in
One, reflect on
the questions
and discuss your
answers with your
study group.

Why do we need to be secure in ourselves before we can understand and respect someone
else's point of view?

_____

_____

_____

_____

_____

_____

What do you think it means for someone to
"give up the right to be offended"?

_____

_____

_____

_____

_____

_____

Study Scripture

Read Matthew 5:43-48:

"You have heard that it was said, 'Love your neighbor and hate your enemy.' But I tell you, love your enemies and pray for those who persecute you, that you may be children of your Father in heaven. He causes his sun to rise on the evil and the good, and sends rain on the righteous and the unrighteous. If you love those who love you, what reward will you get? Are not even the tax collectors doing that? And if you greet only your own people, what are you doing more than others? Do not even pagans do that? Be perfect, therefore, as your heavenly Father is perfect."

What's the difference between sacrificial love and allowing others to walk all over us/becoming a "doormat"?

_____

_____

_____

_____

_____

_____

Why did Jesus command His followers to love their enemies—not just neutral people or casual acquaintances?

_____

_____

_____

_____

_____

_____

How does our love towards others (or lack thereof) indicate the state of our hearts as it relates to God?

_____

_____

_____

_____

_____

_____

Which one of Pastor Dennis's guidelines on having healthy conversations with others stood out to you the most? Why do you think that one in particular caught your attention?

_____

_____

_____

_____

_____

_____

What are some powerful questions you can ask someone who has a different background, race, ethnicity, or belief system than you?

_____

_____

_____

_____

_____

_____

How can the concept of taking time to "cool off" shift the way we navigate conflict as leaders and as believers?

_____

_____

_____

_____

_____

_____

In your own words, what is the "family business" that we've entered into as sons and daughters of God?

_____

_____

_____

_____

_____

_____

_____

Can you think of some examples of times when it's not only okay, but healthy to be angry?

_____

_____

_____

_____

_____

_____

What do you think it looks like to live in a balance between truth and grace? What kind of actions or attitudes accompany someone who has achieved a good balance between the two?

_____

_____

_____

_____

_____

_____

Breaking Down Walls

"We can't manufacture a humble heart. It has to be created in us by a genuine experience of God's grace. If we believe our goodness earns points with God, we'll always look down on people we don't consider as good as we are."

Reading Time

Read Chapter 8: "Breaking Down Walls," in *One*, reflect on the questions and discuss your answers with your study group.

What "bricks in the wall" have you observed that separate people and keep them from experiencing connection and understanding with one another?

_____

_____

_____

_____

_____

_____

What solutions have you found—ways to "break down the walls"—in your own conversations with others?

_____

_____

_____

_____

_____

_____

Study Scripture

Read John 13:1-17:

"It was just before the Passover Festival. Jesus knew that the hour had come for him to leave this world and go to the Father. Having loved his own who were in the world, he loved them to the end.

The evening meal was in progress, and the devil had already prompted Judas, the son of Simon Iscariot, to betray Jesus. Jesus knew that the Father had put all things under his power, and that he had come from God and was returning to God; so he got up from the meal, took off his outer clothing, and wrapped a towel around his waist. After that, he poured water into a basin and began to wash his disciples' feet, drying them with the towel that was wrapped around him.

He came to Simon Peter, who said to him, "Lord, are you going to wash my feet?"

Jesus replied, "You do not realize now what I am doing, but later you will understand."

"No," said Peter, "you shall never wash my feet."

Jesus answered, "Unless I wash you, you have no part with me."

"Then, Lord," Simon Peter replied, "not just my feet but my hands and my head as well!"

Jesus answered, "Those who have had a bath need only to wash their feet; their whole body is clean. And you are clean, though not every one of you." For he knew who was going to betray him, and that was why he said not every one was clean.

When he had finished washing their feet, he put on his clothes and returned to his place. "Do you understand what I have done for you?" he asked them. "You call me 'Teacher' and 'Lord,' and rightly so, for that is what I am. Now that I, your Lord and Teacher, have washed your feet, you also should wash one another's feet. I have set you an example that you should do as I have done for you. Very truly I tell you, no servant is greater than his master, nor is a messenger greater than the one who sent him. Now that you know these things, you will be blessed if you do them."

Jesus answered, "Those who have had a bath need only to wash their feet; their whole body is clean. And you are clean, though not every one of you." For he knew who was going to betray him, and that was why he said not every one was clean.

When he had finished washing their feet, he put on his clothes and returned to his place. "Do you understand what I have done for you?" he asked them. "You call me 'Teacher' and 'Lord,' and rightly so, for that is what I am. Now that I, your Lord and Teacher, have washed your feet, you also should wash one another's feet. I have set you an example that you should do as I have done for you. Very truly I tell you, no servant is greater than his master, nor is a messenger greater than the one who sent him. Now that you know these things, you will be blessed if you do them."

How does Christ model humility without thinking less of Himself, His character, or His talents? Does this passage change your perspective on humility at all?

_____

_____

_____

_____

_____

What differences do you see between the kingdom mindset Jesus demonstrates in this passage and the culture of our world?

_____

_____

_____

_____

How can simplistic solutions actually complicate the process of reconciliation?

_____

_____

_____

_____

In your own words, explain the cycle of distrust and why it's an easy cycle to fall into for so many.

_____

_____

_____

_____

_____

"Many of us have a deeply flawed view of humility. It's not thinking less of ourselves, berating our character and discounting our talents. It's being so secure that we aren't defensive, too eager to please, or afraid of taking a risk."

What qualities or values do you think our culture has idolized today? What about you personally?

_____

_____

_____

_____

_____

_____

How do these "idols" keep us from experiencing reconciliation with others?

_____

_____

_____

_____

_____

_____

_____

Do you have friends from other races who are dear to you—people you truly trust and know? What do you think has contributed to your answer?

_____

_____

_____

_____

_____

_____

_____

What practical steps can you take to pursue more of these relationships?

_____

_____

_____

_____

_____

What are some concrete signs that will tell you when you're making progress in this area?

_____

_____

_____

_____

Stand Up, Speak Up

"In my experience, changing a deeply held conviction requires many, many conversations and experiences. Be patient, be kind, and realize you're asking the person to overcome years of beliefs and habits. If you begin with what you agree on, you have a much better chance of making real progress toward open and honest conversations."

Reading Time

Read Chapter 9: "Stand Up, Speak Up," in *One*, reflect on the questions and discuss your answers with your study group.

Why is it important to be comfortable with "creating sparks," or causing waves, in our efforts toward reconciliation?

_____

_____

_____

_____

_____

_____

What are some of the things we sacrifice by committing to love those of other backgrounds? What do we gain?

_____

_____

_____

_____

_____

Study Scripture

Read Luke 14:25-34:

"Large crowds were traveling with Jesus, and turning to them he said: 'If anyone comes to me and does not hate father and mother, wife and children, brothers and sisters—yes, even their own life—such a person cannot be my disciple. And whoever does not carry their cross and follow me cannot be my disciple.

'Suppose one of you wants to build a tower. Won't you first sit down and estimate the cost to see if you have enough money to complete it? For if you lay the foundation and are not able to finish it, everyone who sees it will ridicule you, saying, "This person began to build and wasn't able to finish."

'Or suppose a king is about to go to war against another king. Won't he first sit down and consider whether he is able with ten thousand men to oppose the one coming against him with twenty thousand? If he is not able, he will send a delegation while the other is still a long way off and will ask for terms of peace. In the same way, those of you who do not give up everything you have cannot be my disciples.

'Salt is good, but if it loses its saltiness, how can it be made salty again? It is fit neither for the soil nor for the manure pile; it is thrown out.

'Whoever has ears to hear, let them hear.'"

What is the "cost" Jesus is really referring to in this passage?

_____

_____

_____

_____

_____

How do you think our cultural Christianity differs from the kind of discipleship Jesus outlines in this passage?

_____

_____

_____

_____

_____

How is white guilt different from loving inclusion? How is it better than white rage?

_____

_____

_____

_____

_____

In your own words, what does it mean to pose a position as a relational issue instead of simply an issue of principle? How does this change the tone and feel of a debate?

_____

_____

_____

_____

_____

What common ground can you find with people who are different than you? Think of a specific demographic that you struggle to understand, and brainstorm a few things you have in common.

_____

_____

_____

_____

_____

_____

According to Pastor Dennis, what are some of the signs that it's time to walk away from a debate and agree to disagree with someone else?

_____

_____

_____

_____

_____

What does it mean to "choose who you lose," and why is this better than not taking a stand at all?

_____

_____

_____

_____

_____

_____

There's a price to pay for standing up for reconciliation, and there's a price to pay if you don't. Why is the latter price often a hidden one? What might be some of the ways we "pay" for not taking a stand?

_____

_____

_____

_____

_____

As you finish this chapter, is there anything you believe God is calling you to do or say? What convictions are you aware of? What relationships are you feeling led to pursue?

_____

_____

_____

_____

_____

I Have a Dream

"A Christian doesn't go with the cultural flow; a Christian goes with the gospel of Jesus, the message of sacrificial love, and a heart out to care for everybody, especially the disadvantaged."

Reading Time

Read Chapter 10: "I Have A Dream," in *One*, reflect on the questions and discuss your answers with your study group.

What's been the number one takeaway you've gotten from doing this study so far?

_____

_____

_____

_____

_____

_____

What's one thing that has challenged you the most, or that you are still wrestling with, as you reach this last chapter?

_____

_____

_____

_____

_____

_____

Study Scripture

Read Romans 12:1-10:

"Therefore, I urge you, brothers and sisters, in view of God's mercy, to offer your bodies as a living sacrifice, holy and pleasing to God—this is your true and proper worship. Do not conform to the pattern of this world, but be transformed by the renewing of your mind. Then you will be able to test and approve what God's will is—his good, pleasing and perfect will.

For by the grace given me I say to every one of you: Do not think of yourself more highly than you ought, but rather think of yourself with sober judgment, in accordance with the faith God has distributed to each of you. For just as each of us has one body with many members, and these members do not all have the same function, so in Christ we, though many, form one body, and each member belongs to all the others. We have different gifts, according to the grace given to each of us. If your gift is prophesying, then prophesy in accordance with your faith; if it is serving, then serve; if it is teaching, then teach; if it is to encourage, then give encouragement; if it is giving, then give generously; if it is to lead, do it diligently; if it is to show mercy, do it cheerfully.

Love must be sincere. Hate what is evil; cling to what is good. Be devoted to one another in love. Honor one another above yourselves."

Identify two or three "active" verbs from this passage that stand out to you. How do these commands go against a passive, complaining mindset when it comes to reconciliation?

_____

_____

_____

_____

_____

_____

_____

_____

Think about those you struggle to get along with or to understand—what spiritual gifts do they possess that you don't have?

_____

_____

_____

_____

_____

What are the main sources of information and entertainment that are informing your heart? Are there any changes you want to make in the places you get content, information, and opinions?

_____

_____

_____

_____

_____

How is the church pivotal to the generational change we want to see in America today? What will we lose if the church isn't leading the charge of reconciliation and equality?

_____

_____

_____

_____

_____

How is it helpful to recognize that human nature will always cause people to be divisive? In other words, if human nature isn't going to change, what's the solution?

_____

_____

_____

_____

_____

_____

Explain what's powerful in the four words, "I see your point." What does this do to the atmosphere of the conversation? Why is this so often a difficult concession for people to make in debates with one another?

_____

_____

_____

_____

_____

_____

Pastor Dennis writes, "Faith comforts, but faith also compels." What is God compelling you to do that is out of your comfort zone?

_____

_____

_____

_____

_____

As you finish this study, what's one area in this topic that you still have questions about?

_____

_____

_____

_____

_____

What resources, people, decisions, or commitments have you made? Make a list of them below, and pray that God will help you in pursuing reconciliation, equality, and peace with others.

_____

_____

_____

_____

9 781950 718573